Fir Trees

Fir Trees

by Heiderose and Andreas Fischer-Nagel

A Carolrhoda Nature Watch Book

 Carolrhoda Books, Inc./Minneapolis

Many thanks to Glenn R. Furnier, Assistant Professor of Forest Biology, and Carl Vogt, Consulting Forester, from the Department of Forest Resources at the University of Minnesota, for their assistance.

To our children, Tamarica and Cosmea Désirée

This edition first published 1989 by Carolrhoda Books, Inc.
Original edition published © 1986 by Kinderbuchverlag KBV Luzern AG,
Lucerne, Switzerland, under the title DER TANNEBAUM.
Copyright © 1986 Kinderbuchverlag KBV Luzern AG.
This edition copyright © 1989 Carolrhoda Books, Inc.
Translated from the German by Mark Lerner.
Adapted by Carolrhoda Books, Inc.

All additional material supplied for this edition © 1989 by
Carolrhoda Books, Inc.

LIBRARY OF CONGRESS CATALOGING-IN-PUBLICATION DATA

Fischer-Nagel, Heiderose.
    [Tannenbaum. English]
    Fir trees/ by Heiderose and Andreas Fischer-Nagel.
      p. cm.
    Translation of: Der Tannenbaum
    "A Carolrhoda nature watch book"
    Includes index.
    Summary: Describes the development and ecosystem
of the endangered fir tree
    ISBN 0-87614-340-0 (lib. bdg.)
    1. Fir—Juvenile literature. 2. Forest ecology—Juvenile
literature. [1. Fir. 2. Trees. 3. Forest ecology. 4. Ecology.]
I. Fischer-Nagel, Andreas. II. Title.
QK494.5.P66F57   1989
585'.2—dc19
                            88-37321
                               CIP
                               AC

Manufactured in the United States of America

1 2 3 4 5 6 7 8 9 10 99 98 97 96 95 94 93 92 91 90 89

For many centuries, fir trees, with their graceful shapes and branches of green, have been a familiar sign of Christmas in many countries of the world.

Fir trees, however, are important for more than just their use as Christmas trees. They provide wood for lumber and paper, homes for animals and other plants, and beautiful scenery for our enjoyment. They also clean the air and prevent the soil from washing away.

This book explains how fir trees grow and reproduce and how you can identify them in the forest. The delicate relationships between firs and other members of the forest and the world are also described. As you read, you will come to understand why fir trees are endangered and what you can do to help save them.

Fir trees are **conifers,** or cone-bearing trees. They are called conifers because their seeds are encased in hard, protective cones. Many of these trees grow into cone-like shapes as well. Coniferous trees are some of the tallest, oldest, slowest-growing, and longest-living beings in the world.

Like all trees, conifers are either **deciduous** or nondeciduous. Deciduous trees lose their leaves in the fall. As the days shorten and the air becomes cool and dry, the trees' moisture and food sugars descend into the roots to be stored for winter. The trees go into a period of **dormancy,** or rest. The leaves change color and dry out or wilt from frost before falling from the trees.

Fir trees, like most other conifers, are evergreens, or nondeciduous trees. Evergreens are active all winter, although their growth slows down. Their leaves, which are needles, remain on the tree year-round, staying green throughout the winter. The needles are narrow and hard, covered by a waxy layer called the **cuticle.** This layer seals in moisture and protects the needles from bitter winds and freezing rain.

Fir trees are not the only evergreens used for Christmas trees. Many other conifers, like spruces, are often chosen. (Fir trees, though, keep their needles and fragrance longest after being cut.) Since spruces look so much like firs, it is often difficult to tell them apart.

Look carefully at the three main trees in the picture to the right. They seem alike, but the middle tree looks slightly bent, its branches dangling at a slant. This is a spruce tree. From far away, its conelike shape is streamlined, tapering smoothly to its top.

The mature firs, though, have more of a spiked look. The branches grow upward at an angle from their trunks. Firs can often be recognized from a distance by their dense, somewhat rounded tops.

Looking closer, you can see that the fir's needles are about 1 to 1½ inches (2.5-3.8 cm) long and flat. (You can remember this characteristic by thinking *flat* means *fir*.) The needles often stick out from the tops of the twigs in two or more rows. If you pluck a single needle from a fir twig, it will come out cleanly, leaving a little hole on the twig.

In contrast, if you pull out one of the spruce's round, pointed needles, it will come off with bits of bark, leaving a torn scar behind. The needles of the spruce are also shorter than those of the fir. They grow to be about 1 inch (2.5 cm) long, arranged evenly on all sides of the twigs. Because the needles of the spruce are sharp to the touch and those of the fir are not, some have nicknamed them "Spiney Spruce" and "Friendly Fir."

The most obvious difference, though, between the two trees is the way their cones grow. The fir's cones grow upright and break apart on the tree in the fall. The spruce's hang from the branches and remain on the tree throughout the winter. They then fall from the tree and break apart on the ground.

To make a final check on whether you have found a fir or a spruce tree, turn the branches over. Two bright bluish white stripes run lengthwise along the underside of most fir needles. Spruce needles are a solid green on both sides.

Fir trees are in the *Pinaceae* family and have the scientific group name *abies.* Throughout the world, 55 **species,** or kinds, of fir trees exist. Most of them live in the northern hemisphere, or half of the globe. They grow well in cool climates and high altitudes, such as in the Soviet Union's Caucasus Mountains. This is where the Nordmann fir (upper left) grows. Yet, some firs live as far south as Guatemala in Central America.

In North America, there are nine species of firs. The Fraser fir is found in the Great Smokey Mountains, and the balsam fir grows just north of these mountains—from the Atlantic Ocean, west along both sides of the northern Great Lakes, through Canada to Alberta. The subalpine fir (cover), grand fir, and white fir (lower left) are found from the Rocky Mountains to the West Coast. In addition to these species, the Pacific Northwest has the noble fir, with its blue-green needles and exceptionally large cones (p. 13 upper left), the Pacific silver fir, and the bristlecone fir. The range of the bristlecone extends north into British Columbia and Alaska.

As a state, California has the greatest variety of naturally growing fir trees. Along with the grand, white, noble, Pacific silver, and bristlecone firs, the state also has the California red fir (above).

Many countries or areas of the world have fir trees named after them. The Greek fir grows in Greece, the Sicilian fir is found on the Italian island of Sicily, and the small Korean fir (to the left) lives in Korea. In the upper European countries, the European silver fir (on page 2) is a familiar sight.

As you look at this five-year-old fir seedling, it is difficult to imagine that the most important chemical reaction in the world is continually taking place within it. Every day this young tree, like other plants, produces its own food from sunlight, air, water, and nutrients from the soil. This process is called **photosynthesis**, which means "putting together with light."

Fir needles, like other leaves, are green because they contain a green substance called **chlorophyll**. Chlorophyll plays a key role in photosynthesis.

Fir needles also have air holes, or **stomata,** which run in two lengthwise rows along the needles' undersides. The stomata take in carbon dioxide for photosynthesis. **Carbon dioxide** is a colorless gas that humans and other animals expel into the air when they breathe out.

At the center of each needle lies a vein that delivers water and nutrients from the roots to all parts of the needle. Water and nutrients are the final ingredients necessary for photosynthesis.

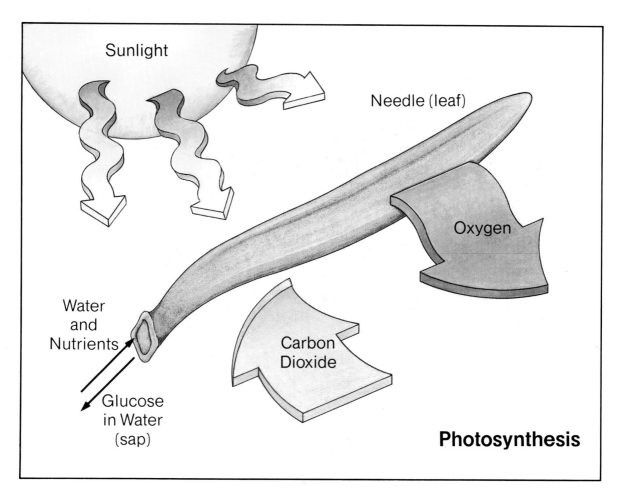

Photosynthesis

In photosynthesis, the needles' chlorophyll absorbs sunlight and turns it into chemical energy. This energy combines the water, nutrients, and carbon dioxide into a sugar called **glucose**. Glucose is the substance the tree uses for food. It dissolves in water and becomes the tree's sap. That is why sap tastes sweet. Glucose is also found in many of the things we eat. If you read the backs of food packages, you will see that we have glucose in several brands of things like peanut butter and ketchup.

As glucose is made, some leftover chemical ingredients are put into the air in the form of **oxygen**—the unseen gas that animals need to live. One of the world's main sources of oxygen is trees. So even though we may not realize it, we depend on trees and other plants for every breath.

Trees do more than just produce oxygen. They also clean and filter the air. As trees take in carbon dioxide, they absorb many harmful substances, such as automobile exhaust; factory smoke; and some dangerous natural gases, like those from erupting volcanoes.

Fir trees, like other conifers, are exceptionally sensitive to air pollution because they keep their needles for years, and pollutants collect in them over time. Some chemical substances can be broken down in the needles, but a buildup of too many pollutants eventually kills the needles' cells. The trees then starve because they can't produce the glucose they need.

Normally, fir needles last 8 to 11 years. They fall from the tree at different times during the year as they wear out. In a tree afflicted by pollution, the needles dry out and die much more quickly.

Another threat to firs, and plants in general, is **acid rain.** When the pollution from some manufacturing plants mixes with water in the air, it forms poisonous rain water. When the rain hits the firs' needles, it can eat away the plants' cells. In addition, the soil can be spoiled and the roots damaged.

A coniferous forest dies slowly. Needles first turn a grayish green or yellow and then change to brown and red. When the tops of the trees thin out, as this fir's has, the evergreens can no longer be saved. They will be dead within a few years.

17

A tree's skin is its bark—thick layers of dead cells. As the tree ages, the outer layers of bark peel off naturally and are replaced from underneath by new layers.

Bark protects the tree from damage. It insulates the tree against extreme temperatures, shields it from dangerous insects and diseases, and prevents water loss. That is why it is so harmful to carve your initials into the trunk of a tree or peel its bark.

Firs, like some other conifers, have an additional defense—**resin**—a fragrant, gummy substance that hardens as it hits the air. In fir trees, resin lies in blisters underneath the bark, in the needles, and at the tips of cones. When fir trees are cut or damaged, resin oozes out and forms a protective crust, closing the wounds.

Because of resin's stickiness, scientists have found many important uses for it. It is an ingredient in healing salves, paints, stains, varnishes, and sealers. Resin cannot be dissolved in water, so once it is on your hands, you need turpentine to wash it off.

Underneath the bark are ringed layers of cells that work as minipipelines. They carry fluids up and down the trunk, between the roots and the leaves. The outer layers of cells, or **phloem** (pronounced FLOW-em), carry the sap from the leaves down to the roots. As phloem cells wear out and die, they harden and become the inside layers of bark. Then, as outside layers of bark fall off, these phloem cells become the exterior bark.

The next layer of cells within the tree is the **cambium** (pronounced CAM-bee-em)—the tree's factory for new cells. All growth in the width of the trunk or branches comes from this single, razor-thin layer of cells. These cambium cells are constantly dividing and subdividing. They send out new cells into both the outer phloem layers and the inner **xylem** (pronounced ZI-lem) layers.

Xylem cells carry water and minerals from the roots to the leaves. As the xylem cells get worn out and clogged with waste materials, such as minerals and extra resin, the cells harden and die. New, living xylem cells are laid over them by the cambium. The older, dead cells become the inner core of the tree.

Cross Section of a Fir Trunk

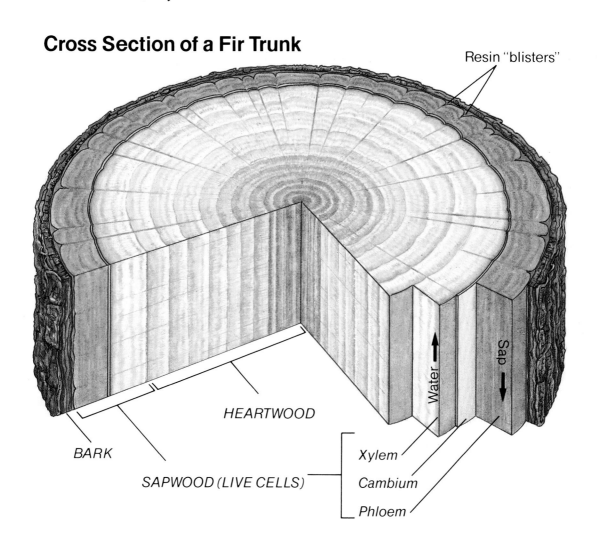

Resin "blisters"

HEARTWOOD

BARK

SAPWOOD (LIVE CELLS)

Water

Sap

Xylem

Cambium

Phloem

The living section of the tree—the phloem, cambium, and xylem cells—is called the **sapwood**. The inner core of the tree—the darker-colored, dead xylem cells—is the **heartwood**. When a tree is young, it is mostly sapwood. As the tree grows older, more of it becomes heartwood.

Heartwood is the tree's backbone, the hardest and oldest part of the tree. As waste deposits build up in the dead cells, the heartwood grows stronger and more rigid. This is the part of the tree cut for lumber. Pound for pound, the heartwood is stronger than steel.

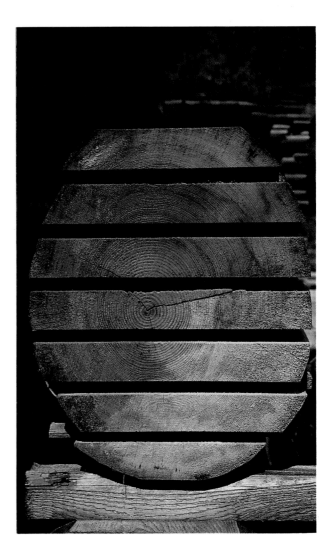

Fir trees, like all conifers, are **softwood** trees. This means that the layers of xylem cells are connected in a honeycomb fashion with side openings. The water and minerals from the roots travel up through the tree in a sideways, zigzag manner. They move from one line of cells to the next and back again. Some water remains in the cells, making the wood generally softer than that of **hardwood** trees.

Hardwood trees have xylem cells that are connected in chains. The watery fluids travel directly from a pit in the bottom of each cell to a pit in the top, and into the bottom of another xylem cell. Hardwood trees seem hard because their xylem cells generally keep less water in them than those of softwood trees. There are, however, some hardwood trees whose wood is softer than most softwood trees' wood.

This fir forest is deeply rooted in the hillside. Anchoring each of these enormous, heavy firs is a main root called the **taproot.** It reaches straight down into the ground, continually growing deeper to supply even the outermost branches with essential water and minerals. Smaller root branches grow off from the taproot. While straining minerals from the soil and sending water to the needles, the roots take hold of the earth and keep the tree stable. Without the roots' tight grasp, the hills and mountains would lose their soil through water runoff, landslides, and avalanches.

As with most trees, the roots are covered by root bark. Underneath the bark are layers of phloem, cambium, and xylem cells that connect with those in the trunk, branches, and twigs. Together, a complete liquid transportation system is formed. Water and minerals flow up from the roots to the needles, and glucose flows down from the needles to the roots.

Fir trees generally start to sprout in May. Buds at the ends of each twig and branch grow green and burst open. Out of them, new twigs, or **shoots,** emerge with soft, light green needles. Throughout the summer, the needles darken until they become a deep, silky green.

The buds that burst this spring were formed last season, and no additional needles or branches will sprout during the summer. The number of buds on each tree depends on the amount of water, nutrients, and sunlight the tree received during the previous year. The conditions of the current summer will only affect the length of the tree's needles and twigs, not how many there are.

Late in the spring, after the needles have sprouted, cone buds form at the far reaches of the top branches. They grow into small male cones. These mushy, golden clumps carry microscopic grains of **pollen** that contain male reproductive cells, or **sperm.**

Farther in along the branches, closer to the fir's trunk, green female cones grow upright. The cones are generally 2 to 6 inches (5.1-15.2 cm) long. Each cone is made up of scales that are connected to an inner pole, or **axis.** On female fir cones, scales usually grow in pairs. Although the two scales look similar, one is merely a woody flap, and beneath the other lies an **ovule.** The ovule is a protective covering for the **eggs,** or female reproductive cells. Nestled under each ovular scale are two egg cells, and underneath them is the non-ovular scale.

Like most conifers, fir trees do not need insects to help them reproduce. As the wind blows through the fir's branches, small grains of pollen blow

off the male cones and land between the soft scales of the female cones. Some grains become trapped by droplets of a sticky liquid on the ovules. The joining of the pollen with the cones is called **pollination.** Once joined, the pollen sends hollow tubes into the ovules. The sperm travel through these tubes to unite with the eggs, a process called **fertilization.**

The fertilized eggs wait in a dormant state until at least the next spring to develop. The amount of time spent in dormancy depends on the species and the amount of rain and sunlight a tree receives.

If enough eggs in a cone are fertilized, the cone eventually develops, growing darker, fatter, and more rigid. Otherwise the cone dries up and falls off the tree.

Although all firs have male and female cones, the cones of various species differ in size and color.

Fir trees have to develop for many years before they are mature enough to produce cones. The exact age depends on the species and the strength of the individual tree. It is usually between 15 and 40 years. After that, new cones are formed every 2 to 7 years, again depending on the species and the individual tree. A great amount of energy is needed for a tree to bring a crop of cones to maturity, so trees often rest a few years between cone-bearing seasons.

In autumn, when the sun is still warm, the firs' cones begin to break apart on the trees, a little at a time, until only the axis of each cone remains. As the cones fall apart, they release seeds. The wind then sweeps these seeds into flight, taking them away.

29

Doesn't it seem amazing that a giant fir can grow from such a small, dry seed?

Inside the seed's casing, the beginning of a plant rests in a dormant state, waiting for the right amount of moisture and sunlight to start it growing. The plant inside the seed can rest there for a long time—even years—until growing conditions are just right.

At first, a little green root stalk pushes its way out of the pointed end of the seed casing, which has become softened with moisture. Guided by gravity, the root stalk grows down into the earth and sends a stem up toward the sun. As it grows, the stem lifts the seed casing into the air, and four to eight long, narrow seed leaves unfold.

The tree sprout you see in the upper left picture is a few weeks old and is between 1 and 2 inches (2.5-5.1 cm) tall. After several more weeks, a second level of green needles grows from this stem. The lower part of the first shoot turns brown and becomes "woody."

Seedlings grow slowly, sending out new rings of needles a little at a time. This little tree sprout has already reached the age of three or four years.

Not every seed grows into a new fir tree. Each fir tree makes hundreds of seeds so that at least a few will someday become new trees. Many seeds are eaten by small animals, like squirrels, rabbits, and mice. Others are blown into lakes and creeks or onto dirt that is baked and dry. Only when a seed falls upon a favorable place, like loose forest soil or between mosses, will it have a chance of growing into a healthy seedling.

These three fir trees are 12 to 15 years old. They are growing too close together for all of them to reach maturity. Each will need more room in the ground for roots and in the air for branches. They may all die, or the hardiest will survive and the others will sicken and eventually die.

To prevent this overcrowding, nature has ways of keeping the number of seedlings in a healthy balance. Many fir seedlings, as well as needles and branches, are eaten by animals. Some become infested with insects and fungi, and others are burned by small fires.

As trees grow, litter collects on the forest floor: dead leaves, pieces of dried bark, worn needles and old cones, fallen trees and broken branches. Many insects, animals, and fungi feed off this litter and make their homes in it.

When the summer is hot and dry, the litter is ideal fuel for fires. If lightning strikes, the forest may blaze into flames. Only the strongest trees, protected by thick bark, will survive. Fire thins out weak trees, giving others room to grow. It also kills many destructive insects and fungi that might otherwise grow out of control.

Small fires, which seem to occur naturally every 10 to 15 years, keep forests healthy. After a fire, sunlight can again reach the forest floor, helping new seedlings and other plants grow. The ash left behind by the fire enriches the soil with nutrients, and some tree species, like jack pine, depend on a fire's heat to reproduce. The heat opens their cones so the seeds fall to the ground and sprout. Foresters often allow these natural fires to burn for the forest's good, yet they watch them carefully so they don't get out of control.

Fire can also be a forest's fiercest enemy. When there haven't been occasional fires to reduce litter, sparks turn more easily into flame. Because of the buildup of materials on the forest floor, the resulting fires spread much more rapidly and burn at higher temperatures. They often destroy even the strongest trees. Each year, raging fires wipe out three million acres (1.2 million hectares) of forest in the United States alone. Most of these fires (90%), though, are not caused by lightning. They are caused by people who do not obey burning rules or are not careful about such things as cigarettes and campfires.

Each forest is a distinct natural environment. The soil is fertilized through the natural processes of animals and plants living together. If a single species in a forest community moves on or dies out—no matter how small or few in number—damage can be caused. The fragile balance of the forest is then thrown off.

For example, red ants build their nests, or anthills, out of needles and twigs. Often called "the forest police," these ants exterminate vast numbers of harmful animals and insects.

In the spring, small aphids multiply on fir trees and other forest plants. They suck on shoots and sprouts without damaging them. The aphids deposit a sweet juice, called honeydew, on the leaves. Red ants like to eat this honeydew, so they protect the aphids. When watched over by the ants, aphids multiply rapidly. The ants can't harvest all the honeydew they produce, so other insects come for their share.

Honeybees swarm to drink the sweet honeydew. The bees then return to their hives to make delicious forest honey. As they travel back and forth, they spread pollen grains, helping many trees, shrubs, and herbs of the forest reproduce.

Not all forests, though, grow naturally. Throughout the world, many public forests are watched over by government officials. These foresters work to make sure the forest is able to provide food and shelter for wildlife; protect the soil; supply wood for fuel and wood products (when needed); and, at times, be a place of relaxation and recreation for visitors.

Foresters are often faced with difficult decisions when the different roles of the forest conflict. For instance, if a camping area is being overused so that seedlings are being trampled and area animals are too disturbed to reproduce, what should be done? The forester may decide to close the section for a season, giving the forest a rest, or limit the number of campers allowed in the area.

Many other forests are owned and managed by companies that make wood products, such as lumber, paper, and fuel. Scientists are constantly developing additional ways to use wood. Cellophane and rayon, as well as some new plastics and foods, are just some examples of these wood products.

Trees grow slowly and, since people use them in so many ways, trees are being cut faster than they can grow. To prevent a shortage, some wood-product companies have begun to grow trees as a crop to be harvested. Conifers are often grown because of the high quality of their wood. Fir trees have a beautiful light brown wood that is used for building homes and small furniture, as well as for making paper.

At tree farms, or nurseries, fir seedlings are started from seeds in greenhouses or outdoor nursery beds. Once they reach a few inches (approximately 7-10 cm) in height, they are planted in fields—in rows like corn or oats. The seedlings above are four years old.

Once the seedlings reach two to four years

of age, they are removed from the fields. They are replanted in a forest area where trees have been cut down. Eventually they outgrow their space and begin to crowd each other. Only 1 out of 10 to 15 planted trees ever grows to be a century (100 years) old. Some are cut for Christmas trees; others sicken and die.

Firs that grow undisturbed in a natural forest can live up to 600 years. They can span more than 5 feet (1.52 m) in diameter and tower over 165 feet (50.3 m) high.

In forests grown for lumber or paper, firs are cut at the age of 140 to 200 years. Their trunks, like that of this fir, soar up 100 to 130 feet (30.5-39.6 m) high and spread out more than 3 feet (1 m) in diameter.

Once a tree is cut, you can tell its age by counting the ringed sections of xylem in the heartwood. A new ring is added each growing season. Every ring around the center represents one year in the tree's life, and the center ring is its first year. The thinner rings indicate summers that were dry with little growth; the thicker rings show those that were wet with abundant growth.

The rings from the growing seasons are separated by darker layers of thinner cells. These cells were made at the end of the growing seasons when there was less activity in the tree and less available water.

We counted the rings in this cut fir and found that the tree started growing in 1823—when James Monroe was president and the United States government was not even 50 years old.

Even though many companies are replanting trees, the world is still losing trees faster than they are being grown. This does not have to happen. We can make better use of our forests. The average American alone uses up two-thirds of an acre (.27 hectare) of forest each year in various tree products—580 pounds (263 kg) of wood just in paper.

If we are careful, we can save trees by wasting less, using only what we need. We can also recycle paper and cardboard instead of throwing them away. Recycling is the process of changing used items back into the materials from which they were made. These materials are then reformed into new products. Making one pound (.45 kg) of paper from recycled products instead of wood saves 17 trees. This method also takes less energy and causes less water and air pollution.

Changes like these in the ways we live make a difference. If we waste less, recycle, and work to keep our air, land, and water free of pollution, we may be able to save our fir trees (and other plants as well). So this year, if you are planning on buying a Christmas tree, consider buying a potted fir tree. When it gets too big, you can plant it in a forest or in your backyard. Maybe 600 years from now, one of your relatives will see this tree and be impressed at its long life.

45

GLOSSARY

acid rain: rain containing a high level of harmful pollutants

axis: the middle stem of a cone

cambium: a single layer of cells between the phloem and xylem that produces new phloem and xylem cells

carbon dioxide: a colorless gas in the air used by plants in photosynthesis

chlorophyll: a green pigment that absorbs sunlight and converts it into chemical energy in photosynthesis

conifer: a scientific order of trees (mostly evergreens) that grow cones

cuticle: the transparent, protective outer layer on coniferous needles

deciduous: a type of tree that loses its leaves every autumn

dormancy: a resting state in which growth stops and activity slows

egg: a female reproductive cell

fertilization: the joining of sperm to egg

glucose: a simple sugar made by plants in photosynthesis and used for food

hardwood: wood with xylem cells that are connected like links in a chain

heartwood: a tree's inner core, made of dead xylem cells

ovule: a protective casing for the egg(s) of a seed plant

oxygen: a colorless gas given off by plants in photosynthesis

phloem: the layers of cells that carry glucose from the leaves to roots

photosynthesis: the process by which a green plant produces glucose from sunlight, water, nutrients, and carbon dioxide

pollen: tiny grains produced by male cones that contain sperm

pollination: the attachment of pollen to a female cone

resin: a gummy liquid that hardens as it meets the air. It protects a tree from damage

sapwood: the living cells of a tree

shoot: a new branch or stem of a plant

softwood: wood with xylem cells that are connected as in a honeycomb

species: a grouping of plants or animals with similar characteristics

sperm: male reproductive cells

stomata: openings in leaves through which water and air pass

taproot: a spikelike main root that grows straight down

xylem: the layers of cells that carry water and nutrients from the roots to leaves

INDEX

ABOUT THE AUTHORS

Heiderose and Andreas Fischer-Nagel received degrees in biology from the University of Berlin. Their special interests include animal behavior, wildlife protection, and environmental control. The Fischer-Nagels have collaborated as authors and photographers on several internationally successful science books for children. They attribute the success of their books to their "love of children and of our threatened environment" and believe that "children learning to respect nature today are tomorrow's protectors of nature."

The Fischer-Nagels live in Germany with their daughters, Tamarica and Cosmea Désirée.

Additional photographs courtesy of: p. 7 (upper right), p. 38, p. 45, Steve Terrill; p. 35, Tony C. Caprio/Breck P. Kent; p. 6, p. 13 (upper right), Glenn Furnier. Front cover, Breck P. Kent. Back cover, Steve Terrill.